IS SINGING FOR YOU?

ELAINE LANDAU

Lerner Publications Company · Minneapolis

Lerner Publications Company
A division of Lerner Publishing Group, Inc.
241 First Avenue North
Minneapolis, MN 55401 U.S.A.

Website address: www.lernerbooks.com

Library of Congress Cataloging-in-Publication Data

Landau, Elaine.
    Is singing for you? / by Elaine Landau.
      p.   cm. — (Ready to make music)
    Includes bibliographical references and index.
      ISBN 978-0-7613-5427-7 (lib. bdg. : alk. paper)
      1. Singing—Instruction and study—Juvenile. I. Title.
    MT898.L36 2011
    783'.043—dc22   2009052350

Manufactured in the United States of America
1 – DP – 7/15/10

CONTENTS

CHAPTER ONE

The Human Voice: A Wonderful Instrument

CHAPTER TWO

So Many Ways to Sing

CHAPTER THREE

Singing and You

CHAPTER FOUR

What Does a Singer Need to Succeed?

4

14

22

28

36   Quiz: Is Singing Right for You?
37   Glossary
37   Source Notes
38   Selected Bibliography
38   For More Information
39   The Singers Who Helped with This Book
40   Index

THE HUMAN VOICE:
A WONDERFUL INSTRUMENT

Picture this:

You're a famous pop singer. Wherever you perform, tickets sell out fast. People see you as a hot new talent. Your voice has been described as phenomenal. Tonight you're singing to a packed house. You start out with a soulful ballad. But you quickly pick up the pace. You can almost feel the electricity in the crowd as you do. You've enjoyed a fast rise to stardom. It's easy to see why. Critics say you have one of the best voices in pop music.

Switch to this scene. This time you're a famous opera singer. Your voice is known for its breathtaking power onstage. It has a heft and beauty all its own. You make the roles you sing come alive.

4

A good pop singer can excite an audience with amazing vocal stylings.

Opera singer Bryn Terfel performs with the Welsh National Opera.

In the past two years, you took Europe by storm. Now you're back in the states. Tonight you're performing to a full opera house. As always, your performance is splendid. You sing with depth and spirit. People say you're fabulous. You're a true opera celebrity.

Can you see yourself in either of these scenes? One great thing about singing is that it allows you to be versatile. Someone with singing talent might sing opera, pop, or a number of other musical styles. For a singer with star potential, the possibilities are endless.

Do you have a passion for singing? Want to learn more about it? If so, keep reading. It's what this book is all about.

SING, SING, SING

There are lots of good reasons to take up singing. If you love to sing, you may have already discovered a few of them. One of the biggest pluses to singing is that it's a wonderful way to express yourself. No instrument is more personal than the human voice. Think about it. Guitarists must pluck strings to make music. Pianists have to strike keys. No strings or keys are involved in singing. It's just you and the audience connecting through your voice.

THE MOST BASIC INSTRUMENT

Not only is the voice personal. It also has a longer history than any other instrument. People were singing long before the flute or the trombone had been invented. Here's how classically trained singer Octavio Orochena put it. "The voice is the most basic instrument. It's the first musical instrument that ever existed. It's been said that all other instruments just imitate the voice."

Many singers love to sing because it lets them connect with an audience.

CONVENIENCE

Do you know anyone who plays a band instrument? Or maybe you're in band yourself. If so, then you know that you need to make sure to remember your instrument on the days when you have band class. If you leave your instrument at home, you'll be out of luck. You'll just have to sit there while your bandmates practice.

Singers never have this problem. They don't need to worry about showing up for rehearsal without their instrument. You always have your voice with you.

In addition, with your voice, there's nothing to carry. Kids who play the clarinet or the trumpet aren't as lucky. And those who play large instruments have it even harder! Ever tried to haul a trombone on the school bus? Singers don't need to worry about toting their instrument around with them.

Band students, unlike singers, need to bring their instruments with them to music classes.

HOW SINGING WORKS — A CLOSE-UP LOOK

What parts of the body do you use when you sing? Perhaps you thought of the mouth and the lungs. After all, you have to breathe to sing—and you have to open your mouth to get that sound out! The mouth and lungs are certainly important. But they're not the only parts of the body that get into the act. Let's take a close-up look at all the parts involved in singing.

TEETH AND TONGUE

The teeth and the tongue affect how you pronounce your words when you sing. Clear pronunciation is important to many singers—especially those who sing classical music. If classical choral singers don't pronounce words clearly, for example, the choir can end up sounding muffled. Audience members may have trouble understanding what they're singing about.

MOUTH

Singers often open their mouths widely when they sing. It helps them to project, or make their voices carry far.

LARYNX AND VOCAL CORDS

Your larynx is located at the top of your windpipe. Your larynx is also known as your voice box. It plays an important role in singing because it holds your vocal cords. You have two pairs of these small bands of tissue. When air from your lungs reaches your lower pair of vocal cords, they vibrate (move back and forth). These vibrations produce the sound you make when you sing.

LUNGS

Breathing deeply puts lots of air into your lungs. Deep breathing is very helpful to singers.

WINDPIPE

Your windpipe allows air
from your lungs to travel to
your vocal cords so they
can vibrate.

DIAPHRAGM

Your diaphragm controls how
much air you use when you sing.
It's a large group of muscles that
stretches directly across the bottom
of your rib cage.

9

COST COUNTS

Lots of instruments are very costly. Even a used tuba or French horn costs more than many families can afford. But your voice is free. It came with your body. Unlike a violin, you never have to buy strings for it. You came fully equipped with vocal cords.

SINGING REALLY WELL

If you can speak, you can sing. But good singers give their audiences much more than that. These singers develop their voices. Their voices are truly musical. It's a pleasure to listen to them.

Singing is a very expressive art.

Sounding great isn't easy. It takes time and hard work. Yet the end result is well worth it. The sound of a great voice can be nearly magical. It can leave almost any audience entranced and wanting more. Opera singer Raffaele Cardone described the power of the human voice this way. "The voice is a natural gift. It's the most precious instrument ever created. With it, we can express all our emotions through song."

A FAMILY OF VOICES

All voices don't sound the same. People sing in different ranges. You can easily hear the difference between male and female voices. But there are further differences within these two groups. Lots of systems for grouping voices exist. So you may have heard different names for different voice types. But the names listed here are the most common ones.

SOPRANO

This is the name for the highest type of voice. Soprano parts are sung by females. Those who sing soprano are not just able to hit the high notes. They are comfortable singing in a high range all the time. Some famous sopranos you may know include Dolly Parton, Sarah Brightman, and Olivia Newton-John.

ALTO

This is the name for the second-highest type of voice. Alto parts are also sung by females. Alto and soprano voices have some similarities. But while sopranos sing the highest notes, altos sing slightly lower parts. Famous altos include Amy Winehouse and Amber Riley (right) from the hit television show Glee.

TENOR

People who sing tenor have a lower voice than altos. Males sing tenor parts. The tenor voice is often described as clear and bright. Justin Timberlake (right) is a tenor. Classically trained singer Josh Groban has sometimes sung tenor parts as well.

BASS

Basses have the lowest singing range. Males sing bass parts too. The bass voice is deep and heavy. Barry White (left) was a bass. Opera singers James Morris and Samuel Ramey are basses.

CHAPTER TWO

SO MANY WAYS TO SING

One day a singer is standing in line for a chance to be on the TV show *American Idol*. Weeks later, the same person is belting out songs onstage. If that singer's *really* lucky, he or she just may be the *American Idol* winner. Then people all over the world may soon know the singer's name.

HAIL, HAIL ROCK AND ROLL

What do *American Idol* singers have in common? All are young and talented. Many are also rock singers. Do you

Many singers dream of making it on American Idol—or, better yet, of winning on the show!

hope to be a rock singer someday? If so, now's a good time to start learning more about rock.

Many different types of music are known as rock. There's soft rock, heavy metal, and pop rock just to name a few. Take some time to listen to different styles of rock. As you listen, picture yourself singing in these different styles. Which fits you best? What do you feel most comfortable with? These are important questions you'll need to answer.

You might also want to think about taking up an instrument. This is often quite helpful to rock singers. Many people think his skill with instruments was a big plus for Kris Allen. Allen became the eighth-season winner of *American Idol* in May 2009. While onstage, he played several different instruments.

Kris Allen of American Idol fame used his varied musical skills to his advantage on the show.

A MULTITALENTED POP STAR

She sings! She dances! She acts! She's the multitalented Jennifer Lopez. This Latina star seems to be good at everything. Her debut pop album was released in 1999. It sold more than a hundred thousand copies within a week. Clearly, Lopez was going to be a major force in pop rock with a Latin flavor.

Lopez's popularity continued to grow. In 2001 her album J. Lo hit number one on the pop charts. Her success has continued to this day. There's no stopping Jennifer Lopez.

Jennifer Lopez has successful careers in both music and movies.

If you do take up an instrument, you might have to spend money on lessons. You may also have to purchase an instrument that you can practice on at home. But if your family can afford these things, taking up an instrument might be worth a try. Being able to accompany yourself is an excellent skill to have. This ability could even boost your chances of performing for an audience someday.

COUNTRY WESTERN MUSIC

Do you love music with a country western flavor? You're not alone. Country western music is extremely popular. It includes everything from slow ballads to upbeat rhythms. And a lot of country music these days has a healthy dose of rock.

If country music is calling to you, listen to a broad range of this music. Try contemporary singers like Taylor Swift and Kenny Chesney as well as older favorites, such as Johnny Cash and Patsy Cline. Zero in on a few of your favorite artists. Study their different styles. Think about how you'd sing the songs they sing.

Country music fans were thrilled when Carrie Underwood won on American Idol.

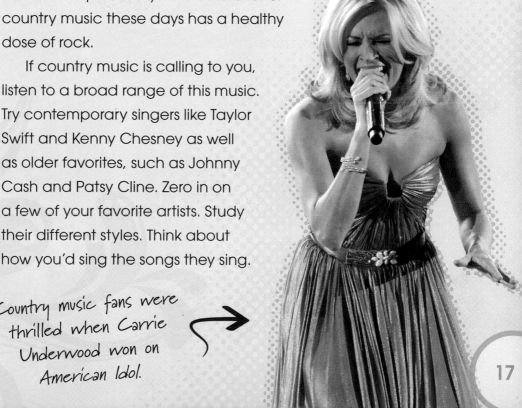

Ella Fitzgerald was one of the greatest jazz artists of all time.

THE JAZZ SINGER

Not everyone is into rock or country music. Some people prefer jazz. Are you among them?

Jazz tends to be less structured than many other types of music. Jazz musicians sometimes make up parts of their music as they perform. This is known as improvisation. It lets musicians really express themselves through their music.

Some jazz singers do scat singing. It's a form of improvisation. In scat singing, singers just sing sounds and syllables. These artists sound like they are performing instrumental solos. But the only instrument they use is their voice.

Would you like to be a jazz singer? Then listen to all the jazz you can. This will give you a better feel for the music. Try singers such as Madeleine Peyroux and Kurt Elling. And don't overlook some of the earlier jazz singers. You can learn a lot from hearing Ella Fitzgerald and Nancy Wilson. Don't forget Louis Armstrong and Scatman Crothers either. Both were known for their scat singing.

CLASSICAL MUSIC

Are you a classy kid who loves classical music? Does the sound of human voices raised in song knock your socks off? If this sounds like you, then you may dream of singing choral music or opera.

Choral singers sing as part of a choir. They might sing Broadway show tunes, traditional carols (especially around the holidays), and Masses. Masses are pieces of music originally written to accompany Christian church services.

Many choirs are split into four sections according to voice type. They have soprano, alto, tenor, and bass sections. Some choirs also include parts for second sopranos and baritones. These singers' ranges fall somewhere in between the four standard ranges.

This boys choir sings carols for the Christmas holiday.

Opera singers perform the Italian opera *Aida*.

If you'd like to sing choral music, sign up for school choir if you haven't already. Or see if there's a choir in your community that you can join. Youth choirs offer wonderful chances for exploring choral music.

Opera singers sing stories set to music. Yet opera's even more than that. It includes drama, costumes, and special effects. Opera singers are part of an exciting art form. Some people say that opera feeds your ears, eyes, mind, and heart.

Do you long to be on the opera stage? If so, learn all you can about opera. Listen to Italian, German, French, and Spanish operas. Be sure to watch some opera DVDs. If live operas take place near where you live, you could even try to go to one. Seeing an opera in person is a great way to learn about opera music.

SOME HELPFUL HINTS
FOR WANNABE SINGERS

No matter what type of music you decide to sing, these handy tips can help you. Give them a try, and prepare to see results!

1. Study the singers you like best. Ask yourself who their audience is. What makes their sound special? You can learn a lot by listening.

2. At the same time, don't try to copy other singers. You'll sound your best if you sing in your own style. It's not usually possible to sing like the pros anyway. As voice teacher Sally Morgan explained, "Most pop singers achieve their sound with help from electronics. If you try to imitate them, you'll be trying to imitate electronics. Instead, just do your best. That's what people will love."

3. Don't smoke, and try to avoid being in smoky areas. Have you ever heard the song "Smoke Gets in Your Eyes"? It can get in your throat too. Smoke can hurt your vocal cords.

4. Try not to yell too much. Yelling can damage your voice. Cheering a little at a concert or a soccer game won't hurt you. Just try not to overdo it!

5. Drink plenty of water. You'll sound better. You just might feel better too. Water is better for you than sugary sodas.

CHAPTER THREE

SINGING AND YOU

You love music and want it to be a big part of your life. You've always felt drawn to singing, and you're pretty sure you'd like to pursue a singing career. But is singing the right choice for you? There's no easy answer to this question. Different people get into singing for different reasons.

Some people begin singing through a choir at school or church. That was the case for singer and music director Gregory D. Sendler. "I've loved singing for as long as I can remember," Sendler said. "I had a first grade teacher who encouraged me. I began singing in

Singing in choir can help you to decide whether singing is right for you. But don't sign up for choir unless you're willing to do the work!

the school choir. I was noticed there and given solos to sing. I continued with my singing through the years. These days, I'm the director of music for a church and its choir."

DON'T START TOO SOON

Learning to sing well is a terrific goal. But it's important not to start any serious training until your voice matures. If you begin training too soon, you could damage your voice.

Girls' voices mature at about the age of fourteen. Boys' voices mature around the age of fifteen. Until then, young singers should not sign up for any type of voice lessons.

Does this mean you have to put off singing for years? No way! There are plenty of ways for you to participate in singing in the meantime. You could sing in school choir. Or join a glee club if your school has one. School musicals provide a great chance for getting involved in singing too. Many churches and community centers also have choirs. Check them out! These groups are wonderful outlets for young people who love singing.

In other cases, kids begin to sing when they get a part in a school musical or play. One famous singer you might know—David Cook—got started in this way. Cook was the seventh-season winner from *American Idol*. In second grade, Cook's teacher gave him a part in a school holiday show. As you might guess, Cook did extremely well. After that, he was in every holiday and PTA show his school had. Thanks to his great talent—and a lot of hard work and luck—he soon went on to bigger and better things.

Other singers were influenced by someone in their family. Jazz singer La Tanya Hall began singing partly because of encouragement from her parents. "My father was a great piano player, and my mother was a singer," she explained. "They instilled (in) me a great passion and a great respect for music. I grew up listening to all the greats, like Sarah Vaughan and Billie Holiday (famous jazz singers). That was probably . . . the greatest gift (my parents) gave to me."

David Cook got started singing after getting a part in a school holiday show.

SPOTLIGHT ON MARC ANTHONY

Singing superstar Marc Anthony (below right) loved music from the time he was young. He showed his singing talent early on. As a child in the Spanish Harlem section of New York City, he used to stand on the kitchen table and sing for his family and neighbors. Those who heard him felt he'd go far. And they were right!

These days, Anthony is sometimes called the King of Salsa. The nickname shows his contributions to salsa music (a Latin American form of music that combines elements of rock, jazz, and rhythm and blues). According to *Guinness World Records*, Anthony is the number one selling salsa artist of all time!

Still other people get into singing just by chance. Maybe a teacher hears them singing in the hall and asks them to try out for a singing group. Or maybe their parents sign them up for a community choir—and they end up loving it!

It's easy to see how someone could fall in love with singing. It's expressive, it appeals to our emotions, and it's a great way to connect to both an audience and other singers. Yet not every kid who starts to sing sticks with it. Singing seriously takes a lot of work. It means memorizing singing parts, learning to sing well with others, and learning to read music if you don't already know how.

So why do some singers stick with singing while others quit? Many longtime singers believe you have to be really passionate about singing. You have to get a great sense of joy out of polishing your voice. Do you feel this way about singing? Do you look forward to opportunities to improve your vocal skills? If so, then singing is probably right for you.

THE RAP ON RAP

Maybe you enjoy singing, but you're just not sure it's your passion. If that's the case, you might want to check out rap. Rap music began in African American communities. Rap combines spoken rhyming lyrics and strong rhythmic music to create an appealing sound.

If you enjoy writing poetry, rap may be the perfect fit. Download a few rap songs or try a rap CD. Will Smith's *Born to Reign* and Lil' Romeo's *Lil' Romeo* are fun choices, and their lyrics are appropriate for listeners of all ages. If you like these albums, try writing some rap of your own. You could even perform your rap songs for your friends and family.

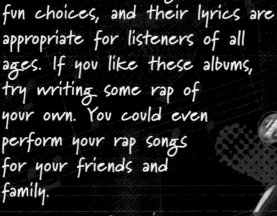

Rapper Jay-Z performs in Los Angeles, California, in 2008.

27

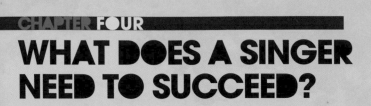

CHAPTER FOUR

WHAT DOES A SINGER NEED TO SUCCEED?

Can you see yourself as an outstanding singer? Do you ever wish that one day you'd just wake up and be great? Audiences would pay to hear you sing, and you'd floor them with your vocal stylings.

This is a wonderful dream, but dreaming alone won't make you a terrific singer. Only you can make that happen. And the only way to get there is through hard work and lots of practice.

PRACTICE MAKES PERFECT

How much should you practice? Well, for now you'll need to practice only if a choir director or school

28

Many singers dream of belting it out before an audience.

musical supervisor needs you to do so. Young singers should limit the amount of time they spend on singing until their voices mature.

But once you're old enough for vocal training, you'll need to practice regularly. Professional singer Victoria Bechtold Kush believes that regular practice is vital for every singer. "You can't expect to sing well if you don't practice," she said. "You must follow a practice routine. You need to do vocal exercises. These help keep your voice in shape. Singers are like athletes. They rely on learned skills. These skills are built up over time. If there's a difficult part of a song, you can't just give up on it. You have to practice it until you get it right."

Singer Victoria Bechtold Kush emphasizes practicing and vocal exercises.

Vocal exercises and warm-ups are important for any serious singer. This high school choir is warming up before a concert.

Some singers practice for hours every day. But you have to be careful. Don't practice so much that you hurt your voice. Your voice isn't like a guitar or a flute. If your voice is badly damaged, you can't go out and buy a new one. As vocal coach Arlene Shrut put it, "Your vocal cords have to last a lifetime. You should always stop singing on any day *before* you get tired."

Many singers look forward to their practice time. They're always striving to improve. As singer Matthew Sabatella said, "I've found that there's no point at which you become good enough. You can always improve. I thought I was a good singer when I was fifteen. Today I think I sing better than I ever have. But I plan to get even better in the future."

A HUMAN BEATBOX

Can you make all sorts of sounds with your mouth? Lots of kids do this for fun. But some people have taken it a step further. They've learned to use their mouth, lips, and tongue to create musical sounds.

Sometimes these musicians sound like a drum. Other times, they almost sound like a whole band. Many combine singing with the sounds they produce. The end result is a new musical art form. It's called beatboxing.

Some beatboxers have albums you can download or CDs you can buy. You can also see beatboxers on YouTube. In addition, you can hear beatboxing on certain pop songs. For instance, Michael Jackson added his own sounds to his song "Billie Jean."

Does beatboxing appeal to you? Then check out music that features beatboxers. Who knows? You may soon be doing some beatboxing of your own!

Darren Foreman, also known as Beardyman, has made a career of beatboxing. This guy has skills!

Accomplshed singers can calmly handle almost any situation onstage.

SURVIVING ONSTAGE

Even if you practice hard and always try your best, things can still go wrong during a performance. Singers can miss notes. They can forget their lyrics. Crazier things can happen too. There might be a power outage onstage. All of a sudden, you're standing in the dark. To make matters worse, your microphone doesn't work! At times, singers have tripped onstage. Some have even fallen off the stage.

Outdoor performances are known to be troublesome. The wind has blown away sheet music. Performers have been soaked in sudden thunderstorms. Insects have even flown into singers' mouths as they sang.

Singer Marisa Molina described some things that have happened to her while performing. "Once I was singing onstage, and a binder filled with sheet music fell off the music stand. Another time somehow a chair was left behind me onstage. It shouldn't have been there, but it was. I accidentally kicked it over, and it landed with a thud!"

Singer Tim Evanicki also experienced a mishap while onstage. He described his experience this way.

POLISH THOSE PEOPLE SKILLS

More than a good voice is needed to succeed as a singer. You need good people skills too. Singers don't work alone. If you sing in a choir, you'll be working closely with lots of other singers. The same goes for students who sing in musicals. And someday, a vocal coach, an employer, and even an agent may come into the picture.

A few simple rules will help you early on. Be on time for rehearsals. Know your material really well. Listen closely to your coach or director. And always treat your fellow musicians with respect.

No matter how talented you are, don't demand star treatment for yourself. No one wants to work with a difficult person. Instead, learn to listen and make friends. Combine people skills with talent and hard work, and you'll be sure to go far.

I was singing at a benefit concert. There were two thousand people in the audience. I had on a white robe that I was supposed to take off. The idea was to show that I was dressing for a date underneath it.

But things didn't go as planned. The robe caught on my pants. It made them fall down around my ankles. I was left onstage showing my boxer shorts to two thousand people. I had to hobble to the microphone. To top it all off, I tripped on my pants and fell flat on my face. It didn't end there either. They kept replaying the concert on TV. It was on about twice a week for a month!

WORDS OF WISDOM

Singer Octavio Orochena had these words of wisdom to offer young singers. "Success in singing doesn't come easily. It can be a long process. Don't rush things. Take one step at a time. You're not going to get every job you try out for. Don't let it get you down. They may be looking for a different type of voice. Just be prepared, and always do your best."

So what do you do when these things happen? You smile and do your best to go on. Remember that sooner or later, performance mishaps happen to everyone. These problems don't make you any less of a singer. Besides, audiences tend to be very forgiving when they're listening to beautiful music.

SUCCESS!

Whether or not your performances are perfect, remember to focus on the music. That's all that really matters in the end. If you give your all to your music and your singing, you can consider your efforts a success! You will have invested time and passion in a worthy goal— expressing yourself through song. For many singers, there's nothing better.

Nothing can beat the sense of pride you'll feel if you work hard to express yourself through song.

QUIZ: IS SINGING RIGHT FOR YOU?

Which of these statements describes you best? Please record your answers on a separate sheet of paper.

1. **When you think of your voice as an instrument,**
   A. You like the idea. The possibility of using your voice to connect to an audience appeals to you.
   B. You think it sounds OK—but what you'd *really* like to do is play the drums or clarinet. You feel you can produce a broader range of sounds with those instruments.

2. **When you hear a good piece of music,**
   A. You really get into all the sounds. You feel as if you could listen to the piece forever!
   B. You think it sounds good, but you don't usually get too absorbed in it. You'd rather spend time working on art or learning new soccer moves than listening closely to music.

3. **You know that formally training your voice too early can damage it. So,**
   A. Right now you're happy singing in school choir. You believe there's plenty of time to get serious about a singing career.
   B. You want to begin your music career right away. You've heard of kids younger than you who've done quite well playing piano or violin. You feel your talent in music might be better directed by learning to play an instrument.

4. **When you're working toward a long-term goal,**
   A. You tend to be patient. Practicing a skill again and again doesn't bother you.
   B. You get a little antsy. You'd rather move on to something new than focus on the same task for a long time.

5. **When you think about practicing your singing,**
   A. You get really excited. You think studying singing sounds like fun!
   B. You like music, but you can think of other things you'd rather do. Giving up free time to practice doesn't sound worth it.

Were your answers mostly As?

If so, singing may just be the right choice for you!

GLOSSARY

alto: the second-highest type of voice

bass: the lowest type of voice

diaphragm: a large group of muscles that stretches directly across the bottom of your rib cage. Your diaphragm controls how much air you use when you sing.

improvisation: making up parts of the music you are performing while you are performing it

jazz: a form of music characterized by loose structure and improvisation

larynx: the upper part of the windpipe. Your larynx holds your vocal cords.

opera: a play in which all or most of the words are sung

pop: an upbeat form of rock music that often appeals to young people. *Pop* is short for popular.

scat singing: a form of improvisation in which singers sing sounds and syllables

solo: a musical performance in which a musician performs alone

soprano: the highest type of voice

tenor: the second-lowest type of voice

vocal cords: four small bands of tissue in the larynx. You have two pairs of vocal cords. When air from your lungs reaches your lower pair of vocal cords, they vibrate and produce sound.

SOURCE NOTES

6   Octavio Orochena, interview with author, June 22, 2009.

11   Raffaele Cardone, e-mail message to author, November 11, 2009.

21   Sally Morgan, telephone conversation with author, November 13, 2009.

22–23   Gregory D. Sendler, interview with author, June 10, 2009.

24 La Tanya Hall, quoted in Ren Media Publishing, "Jazz Monthly.com Feature Interview: La Tanya Hall," interviewed by Baldwin "Smitty" Smith, Jazz Monthly.com , March 2009, http://www.jazzmonthly.com/artist_hp/hall_latanya/interview/latanya_hall.html (March 5, 2010).

29 Victoria Bechtold Kush, e-mail message to author, October 27, 2009.

30 Arlene Shrut, e-mail message to author, September 21, 2009.

30 Matthew Sabatella, e-mail message to author, May 27, 2009.

32–33 Marisa Molina, interview with author, June 16, 2009.

34 Tim Evanicki, e-mail message to author, November 11, 2009.

34 Orochena.

SELECTED BIBLIOGRAPHY

Chapman, Janice. *Singing and Teaching Singing: A Holistic Approach to Classical Voice.* San Diego: Plural Publishing, 2005.

Hamady, Jennifer. *The Art of Singing—Discovering and Developing Your True Voice.* Milwaukee: Hal Leonard Corporation, 2009.

Phillips, Kenneth H. *Teaching Kids to Sing.* New York: Schirmer, 1996.

Phillips, Pamelia S. *Singing for Dummies.* New York: Wiley Publishing, 2003.

FOR MORE INFORMATION

Kenney, Karen Latchana. *Cool Rock Music: Create and Appreciate What Makes Music Great!* Edina, MN: Abdo, 2008. This book introduces rock music and all the different types of rock.

Krohn, Katherine. *Michael Jackson: Ultimate Music Legend.* Minneapolis: Lerner Publications Company, 2010. Read the engaging life story of Michael Jackson, one of the most accomplished singers and performers of all time.

Musicians, Singers, and Related Workers: Bureau of Labor Statistics
http://www.bls.gov/oco/ocos095.htm
Learn all about careers in singing and music at this informative website.

PBS Kids: Jazz
http://pbskids.org/jazz
Check out this site to learn more about jazz. Don't miss the Jazz Greats section, which profiles talented jazz musicians such as Billie Holliday and Louis Armstrong.

THE SINGERS WHO HELPED WITH THIS BOOK

This book could not have been written without the help of these very talented and generous singers.

RAFFAELE CARDONE
Italian tenor Raffaele Cardone has performed in opera and concert houses worldwide. He serves as the artistic director of the Miami Lyric Opera.

TIM EVANICKI
Tim Evanicki studied at the Juilliard School and the Eastman School of Music. He's performed at Carnegie Hall, the Metropolitan Opera, and the Kennedy Center.

VICTORIA BECHTOLD KUSH
Former Miss America contestant Victoria Bechtold Kush has sung in concert venues before many important leaders.

MARISA MOLINA
Marisa Molina is a classically trained singer performing in the South Florida area.

SALLY MORGAN
Sally Morgan is a singer, voice teacher, and actress. She's been an innovator in the field of voice training for more than twenty-five years.

OCTAVIO OROCHENA
Octavio Orochena is a classically trained singer who was formerly with the Opera Pasadena in California.

MATTHEW SABATELLA
Matthew Sabatella is a singer who plays the guitar, the banjo, and the mountain dulcimer. He uses traditional folk music to inspire people, get them singing, and help them better understand people and events from the past.

GREGORY D. SENDLER
Gregory D. Sendler has a master's degree from the New England Conservatory. He's the music director for the Saint John Neumann Catholic Church in Miami, Florida.

ARLENE SHRUT
Arlene Shrut was a Fulbright Scholar in Germany for vocal coaching. She teaches at the Juilliard School and the Manhattan School of Music. She is also the founder of the educational organization the New Triad for Collaborative Arts.

INDEX

alto, 12–13, 19
American Idol, 14–15, 24

bass, 13, 19
beatboxing, 31
Broadway, 19

choral music, 19–20
classical music, 8, 19–20
country music, 17

diagram, 8–9
diaphragm, 9

Glee, 12

instruments, 6–7, 10, 15, 17

jazz, 18, 24

larynx, 8
Latin music, 16, 25

musicals, 24, 33

opera, 4–5, 11, 19–20

performing, 32–35
practicing, 28–30

rap, 27
rock music, 14–15

scat singing, 18
soprano, 12, 19

teeth, 8
tenor, 13, 19
tongue, 8

vocal cords, 8, 10, 21, 30

windpipe, 9

PHOTO ACKNOWLEDGMENTS

The images in this book are used with the permission of: © Sidewaysdesign/Dreamstime
.com, pp. 1, 3; © Jason Stitt/Shutterstock Images, pp. 4-5, 28; © Robbie Jack/CORBIS,
p. 5; © Bvdc/Dreamstime.com, p. 6; © iStockphoto.com/Gustaf Brundin, p. 7; © Laura
Westlund/Independent Picture Service, p. 9 (diagram); © RubberBall/Alamy , p. 9; © Corbis/
Photolibrary, pp. 10, 22; © Steve Skjold/Alamy, p. 11; AP Photo/Scott Gries/PictureGroup,
p. 12; AP Photo/Matt Sayles, pp. 13 (top), 27; © David Redfern/Redferns/Getty Images,
p. 13 (bottom); AMERICAN IDOL PROD./19 TELEVISION/FOX TV NETWORK/FREMANTLE MEDIA
NORTH AMERICA / THE KOBAL COLLECTION, pp. 14-15; AP Photo/Disney, Mark Ashman,
p. 15; AP Photo/Mary Altaffer, p. 16; © Jeff Kravitz/Film Magic/Getty Images, p. 17; AP Photo/
Bob Galbraith, p. 18; © Waltraud Grubitzsh/dpa/CORBIS, p. 19; © EmmePi Travel/Alamy,
p. 20; © Corbis/Photolibrary, p. 22; © Paha_l/Dreamstime.com, p. 23; © Jamie McCarthy/
WireImage/Getty Images, p. 24; © JC Olivera/Latin Content/Getty Images, p. 25; © Ranier
Holz/Photolibrary, p. 26; AP Photo/George Widman, p. 29; © Dean Berry/Photolibrary, p. 30;
© Daniel Walla/Alamy, p. 31; © Ken Schulze/Shutterstock Images, p. 32; © clearviewstock/
Shutterstock Images, p. 35.

Front Cover: © Sidewaysdesign/Dreamstime.com (front); © Peter_g /Dreamstime.com,
(background).